We Are The Champions

We Are The Champions

Champions

A Collection of Sporting Verse
Compiled by Caroline Sheldon and
Richard Heller
Illustrated by Virginia Salter

Hutchinson
London Melbourne Auckland Johannesburg

First published in 1986 by Hutchinson Children's Books Ltd
An imprint of Century Hutchinson Ltd
Brookmount House, 62–65 Chandos Place, Covent Garden,
London WC2N 4NW

Century Hutchinson Publishing Group (Australia) Pty Ltd
16–22 Church Street, Hawthorn, Melbourne, Victoria 3122

Century Hutchinson Group (NZ) Ltd
32–34 View Road, PO Box 40–086, Glenfield, Auckland 10

Century Hutchinson Group, (SA) Pty Ltd
PO Box 337, Bergvlei 2012, South Africa

Set in Plantin by BookEns, Saffron Walden, Essex

Printed and bound in Great Britain by Anchor Brendon Ltd, Tiptree

British Library Cataloguing in Publication Data

We are the champions: a collecton of sporting verse.
    1.   Sports — Poetry   2.   English poetry
    1.   Sheldon, Caroline   2.   Heller, Richard
    821'.008'0355   PR1195.5/

ISBN 0 09 163470 9

Introduction

These are poems about sport–playing it, watching it, being part of it and even hating it! Some are about sporting heroes, some are about sporting disasters; some are about sport at its most serious, some are about sport at its silliest. But whether humorous or serious, all of the poems capture a particular moment or mood that reflects the feelings of triumph, disaster and pure fun that are part of sport.

We hope you enjoy them.

C.S.
R.H.

The Rovers

My Dad, he wears a Rovers' scarf,
He wears a Rovers' cap,
And every Saturday before
He goes to see them fail to score,
  He sighs, 'Oh no!
  Why *do* I go?
  They haven't got –
  They've really not –
A rat's chance in a trap!'

And sure enough
They always stuff
  The Rovers.

My Dad, he wears a Rovers' tie,
  Two huge rosettes as well,
And every time before he leaves
He sits and hangs his head and grieves:
  'I must be mad –
  They're just so BAD!
  They haven't got –
  They've really not –
A snowball's hope in hell!'

And sure enough
They always stuff
  The Rovers.

Rovers' ribbon, Rovers' rattle,
Dad takes when he's off to battle:
Shouts and stamps and stomps and rants.
DAD'S GOT ROVERS' UNDERPANTS!

Rovers' eyes!
Rovers' nose!
Rovers' elbows!
Off he goes

*And sure enough
They always stuff
    The Rovers.*

EXCEPT
One glorious day,
It didn't work that way . . .
This was the state of play . . .

8

A goal-less draw,
But just before
The final whistle went,
Rovers stole
The only goal:
I can't say it was *meant*:

What happened was
A wobbling cross
Back-bounced off someone's bum –
And Praise the Lord!
Rovers scored!
They'd won! Their hour had come!

So Dad, he whirled his Rovers' scarf,
  He hurled his cap up high.
'Oh, we're the best there's ever been!
We're magic!' he yelled out. 'You've seen
  Nothing yet.
  Just wait. We're set!
  Yes, you can bet
  The lads will get
Promotion by and by!

  Our luck is in –
  We're *bound* to win –
    Us Rovers!'

It didn't work that way,
Alas for Dad.
That goal's the only goal
They've ever had.

Now every Saturday before
He goes to see them lose once more,
  He sighs, 'Oh no!
  Why *do* I go?
  They've got a curse –
  They're getting *worse* –
How *can* they be so bad?'

And sure enough
They always
STUFF THE ROVERS!

Kit Wright

Rythm

They dunno how it is. I smack a ball
right through the goals. But they dunno how the words
get muddled in my head, get tired somehow.
I look through the window, see. And there's a wall
I'd kick the ball against, just smack and smack.
Old Jerry he can't play, he don't know how,
not now at any rate. He's too flicking small.
See him in shorts, out in the crazy black.
Rythm, he says, and ryme. See him at back.
He don't know nuthing about Law. He'd fall
flat on his face, just like a big sack,
when you're going down the wing, the wind behind you
and crossing into the goalmouth and they're roaring
the whole great crowd. They're up on their feet cheering.
The ball's at your feet and there it goes, just crack.
Old Jerry dives – the wrong way. And they're jeering
and I run to the centre and old Bash
jumps up and down, and I feel great, and wearing
my gold and purpel strip, fresh from the wash.

Iain Crichton Smith

Denis Law

I live at 14 Stanhope Street,
Me Mum, me Dad and me,
And three of us have made a gang,
John Stokes and Trev and me.

Our favourite day is Saturday;
We go Old Trafford way
And wear red colours in our coats
To watch United play.

We always stand behind the goal
In the middle of the roar.
The others come to see the game –
I come for Denis Law.

His red sleeves flap around his wrists,
He's built all thin and raw,
But the toughest backs don't stand a chance
When the ball's near Denis Law.

He's a whiplash when he's in control,
He can swivel like an eel,
And twist and sprint in such a way
It makes defences reel.

And when he's hurtling for the goal
I know he's got to score.
Defences may stop normal men –
They can't stop Denis Law.

We all race home when full time blows
To kick a tennis ball,
And Trafford Park is our backyard,
And the stand is next door's wall.

Old Stokesey shouts, 'I'm Jimmy Greaves,'
And scores against the door,
And Trev shouts: 'I'll be Charlton,' –
But I am Denis Law.

Gareth Owen

Ghostly Football

As played by the phantoms at Shrule,
Midnight football is eerie and cruel;
If one kicks a ghost
Past the other's goal post,
He wins credit for scoring a ghoul.

Anon

Goalkeeper's Lament

Pass the ball
over here
Pass the ball
over here

Down the field
down the wing
carried on a roar
as supporters sing

A wasted chance
that I could see
why didn't you pass
the ball to me?

It's my turn
I want a kick
I want the crowd to shout my name
Their defence
will look so sick
Who said football's 'just a game'?

I'm a goalkeeper
I hate this role
Pass the ball –
I'll score a goal!

Danny Pollock

I'll Stand the Lot of You

I'll stand the lot of you, I said
to the other kids. They said: Right!

I was Wolves 1957-58:
Finlayson; Stuart, Harris; Slater, Wright, Flowers;
Deeley, Broadbent, Murray, Mason, Mullen.
The other kids were Rest of the World:
Banks; Pele, Best; Best, Pele, Pele;
Best, Pele, Charlton, Pele, Best.
Jimmy Murray kicked off for Wolves.

Wolves were well on top in the opening minutes,
then Rest of the World broke away and scored
seven lucky goals. Wolves were in trouble!
But then tragedy struck Rest of the World:
Pele had to go and do their homework!
They were soon followed by Best and Charlton.
It was Wolves versus Banks!
Now Wolves played like a man possessed.
Soon they were on level terms!
Seven-all, and only minutes to go,
when suddenly – sensation! Banks went off
to watch the Cup Final on television!
Seconds later, a pinpoint Mullen centre
found Peter Broadbent completely unmarked
in front of goal. What a chance!

   He missed it,

and Wolves trooped sadly off towards their bike.
Martin Hall

Big Jim

When we play cricket, we don't let Jim bowl;
And when we play baseball, we don't let Jim bat.
But when we play football, we put Jim in goal,
For balls can't get past him, because Jim's so fat.

Colin West

A Hero

My hero is D. Dougan
He wears old gold and black.
He goes through all defenders,
He leads the Wolves' attack.

He scores in nearly every game.
He thrills the North Bank choir.
He kicks the ball right through the net,
Just like a ball of fire.

John Lane (aged 12)

Cyril the Centipede

Cyril the Centipede
Loved playing games,
And his favourite one was football.
And when he played goal
With nine fleas and a mole
Nothing got past him at all.
They played spiders and newts
But his hundred boots
Gave his team very little to do
And the fleas would get bored,
The mole never scored
And the crowd would just stand there and boo.
'Til one awful day, the crowd stayed away
And no fans for either side came,
But all said and done
When it's none none none none
It's really not much of a game.
Then Cyril the Centipede
Hurt his back leg,
The hundre'th one down on the right.
So he used a small stick
And went 99 click,

Now I'm happy to say it's all right,
But he doesn't play goal
Any more – he's retired
Unbeaten, for nobody scored.
Now he just referees
For the spiders and fleas,
And even the mole
Has just scored.

Jeremy Lloyd

Here are the Football Results

League Division Fun
Manchester United won, Manchester City lost.
Crystal Palace 2, Buckingham Palace 1
Millwall Leeds nowhere
Wolves 8 A cheese roll and had a cup of tea 2
Aldershot 3 Buffalo Bill shot 2
Evertonill, Liverpool's not very well either
Newcastle's Heaven Sunderland's a very nice place 2
Ipswich one? You tell me.

Michael Rosen

Lizzie

When we went over the park
Sunday mornings
We picked up sides.

Lizzie was our centre-forward
Because she had the best shot.

When the teachers
Chose the school team
Marshie was our centre-forward.

Lizzie wasn't allowed to play,
They said.

So she watched us lose instead ...
Michael Rosen

Choosing Sides

First you stand in a bunch
Then it's decided
– though everybody already knows it –
that Rolf and Erik are going to choose
Rolf stands on one line
Erik stands on another
All of us others sit down by the fence
'Lars!' calls out Rolf
'Harold!' yells Erik
'Emil!' 'Kent!' 'David!' 'Thomas!' 'Martin!'
Then it's only me left;
I go to Erik's team
that's already started dribbling the ball . . .

Siv Widerberg

Kitchen Conversation

What've you been doing, this afternoon, Son?
Rolling in mud? – Thumping a lad?
Knocking seven bells out of several lads? – I see!
(Just move over while I mash the tea!)

What were you saying? – Tell me then!
(Pass that bread over here for a minute!)
He nearly knocked your teeth out? – Why?
It's a bit much in school time, Son, innit?

Was there a teacher there?
(Take your boots off the table – they're muddy!)
Yes? – Well, what did he say? –
Oh, I see! – You were playing at Rugby!

Pat Cutts

23

Big Arth

Big Arth from Penarth
was a forward and a half.
Though built like a peninsula
with muscles like pink slagheaps
and a face like a cheese grater
he was as graceful and fast
as a greased cheetah.

A giraffe in the lineout
a rhino in the pack
he never passed forward
when he should've passed back
and once in possession
slalomed his way
through the opposition.

And delicate?
Once for a lark
at Cardiff Arms Park
Big Arth
converted a soft-boiled egg
from the halfway line.

No doubt about it, he was one of
the best players in the second team.

Roger McGough

A Bit of a Ballad

Scotland v. Australia, Murrayfield,
18 December 1981

Oh, broken, broken was the play!
And blawn the half-time whistle!
The Wallabies hae scored tries three,
Four penalties the Thistle.

The second half now gars begin,
On the snaw-stripit green,
And but the twelve points the braw Scots hae,
The Wallabies fifteen.

But 'tis the bonny Andy Irvine
That kicks the penalty
That levels a', 15–15,
As level as your e'e.

And they hae ta'en the whisky malt
That stand to see the battle,
And syne they harry the Scottish team,
As drovers harry cattle!

The lions on the standards roar,
And Scotland scores again!
'Tis the muckle Rutherford –
A drappit goal, ye may ken!

'Hauld fast! Hauld fast!' Clerk Irvine cries,
'My bonny lads, wi' me!
We'll weill withstand, on either hand,
The assaults o' the enemie!'

The Wallabies are ravenous,
They sling the ba' aboot –
The Scots defence stands firm as rock,
They dinna care a hoot!

There's but five minutes' playing time,
Australians leap and rin,
And 'tis gowd jerseys everywhere,
Like a rugby loony-bin!

But 'tis the muckle Rutherford
Has ta'en the ba' in's hands
And kicked it full high i' the freezing air
And higher than the stands.

The ba' has landed on its point,
The ba' has bounced full high –
And tis the wee Renwick has caught it and
'Tis an inescapable try!

Oh, wae, wae, were the Wallabies,
Baith here and owre the faem,
Tae see the braw wee Renwick rin
And bear the victory hame!

For now tis 15–22 –
Australia does trail,
A score that hurts, Irvine converts,
Like driving in a nail.

And so rejoice in Embro toun,
The final whistle blaws,
Mak merrie, 24–15!
All Scots, they hae guid cause.

Gavin Ewart

The Old Field

The old field is sad
Now the children have gone home.
They have played with him all afternoon,
Kicking the ball to him, and him
Kicking it back.

But now it is growing cold and dark.
He thinks of their warm breath, and their
Feet like little hot water bottles.
A bit rough, some of them, but still ...

And now, he thinks, there's not even a dog
To tickle me.
The gates are locked.
The birds don't like this nasty sneaking wind;
And nor does he.

D. J. Enright

Cricketer

Light
as the flight
of a bird on the wing
my feet skim the grass
and my heart seems to sing:
'How green is the wicket.
It's cricket.
It's spring.'
Maybe the swallow
high in the air
knows what I feel
when I bowl fast and follow
the ball's twist and bounce.
Maybe the cat
knows what I feel like, holding my bat
and ready to pounce.
Maybe the tree
so supple and yielding
to the wind's sway
then swinging back, gay,
might know the way
I feel when I'm fielding.

Oh, the bird, the cat and the tree:
they're cricket, they're me.

R. C. Scriven

A Sporting Knock

'Leg stump, please.' The wicket feels hard.
Umpire wakes up to give me my guard.
Blistering pace from the bowler, who's fast,
Eye on the ball if I'm going to last.
I look round the field. Have they left a quick single?
Bowler runs in and my feet start to tingle.
Ball's on its way. (I feel slightly sick.)
Play safe and push forward . . . gosh, that was quick!
Just past the stumps; the bowler looks vexed.
Forget all about it; wait for the next.
I see this one clearly; it's wide and it's high.
A smile of disdain as I let it go by.
The next one's a bouncer: I take a good look.
I'm here for the day; it's too early to hook.
Ball on the way again. (Try not to fiddle,
Make sure you get forward.) Ah, right in the middle.
That sounded sweet. I'm now in control.
Batting today is an absolute stroll,
Total command with each stroke I'll be making,
A hundred, or two, are just there for the taking.
The next ball, I know, will just sit up and beg;
Here comes a boundary . . . ow, that's my leg.
From six miles behind I'm aware of a shout.

Don't be ridiculous, that can't be out.
It was miles off the wicket and terribly high
(I remember at once to start rubbing my thigh).
I glance down the pitch but only to find
A finger well raised . . . that umpire's blind.
A lousy appeal, those fieldsmen are cheaters.
My bat hits the wall from a range of ten metres.
My Captain (the twit) comes and mutters 'Bad luck'.
The idiot scorer says 'Was it a duck?'
I'm going to sulk, I don't care if they see.
'No. Thank you. I really don't want any tea.'
The Captain's made fifty? I couldn't care less.
Starting tomorrow, I'm taking up chess.

Richard Heller

A Somerset CCC Shanty

Bonny Botham my oh me
hit the ball at ten to three
didn't come down 'til after tea
Bonny Ian Botham

Jeff Cloves

The Old Man from Bengal

There was an old man of Bengal
Who purchased a bat and a ball,
Some gloves and some pads;
It was one of his fads.
For he never played cricket at all.

F. Anstey

I Ran for a Catch

I ran for a catch
With the sun in my eyes, sir,
Being sure of a 'snatch'
I ran for a catch ...
Now I wear a black patch
And a nose *such* a size, sir,
I ran for a catch
With the sun in my eyes, sir.

Coulson Kernahan

The Cricket Ball Charm

Now Now
little
Cricket ball
hear me as I
Speak.

Little round shiny
ball ball
With a whee
and a spin
knock those
Stumps as high
as the Sky.

William Paul Olhausen (aged 10)

Quick Ball Man
for Michael Holding

Bowlerman bowlerman –
o such a wheel-action is quick ball man!

A warrior man
das such an all-right movement man.

All day him run races,
a-run those poundin riddim paces.

An wickit dem a-fly like bullit hit dem.
Ball a-hit batsman leg cos it a-fool him.

Batsman a-get caught.
More a-go fi nought.

Pad-up man dem come wid runs in dem head
but dem jus a-come to walk back dead.

An bowlerman is noh jus bowlerman.
De man turn heself now in-a batsman.

An him noh wahn one-one run fi get match fix.
Him only wahn six back-a six.

Soh him noh loveless.
Hug-up regula fram all de mates.

Bowlerman bowlerman –
o such a wheel-action is quick ball man.

James Berry

The Song of Tilly Lally

O, I say, you Joe,
Throw us the ball!
I've a good mind to go
And leave you all.
I never saw such a bowler
To bowl the ball in a tansy
And clean it with my hankercher
Without saying a word.

That Bill's a foolish fellow;
He has given me a black eye.
He does not know how to handle a bat
Any more than a dog or a cat;
He has knock'd down the wicket,
And broke the stumps,
And runs without shoes to save his pumps.

William Blake

Missed

The sun in the heavens was beaming.
The breeze bore an odour of hay,
My flannels were spotless and gleaming,
My heart was unclouded and gay;
The ladies, all gaily apparelled,
Sat round looking on at the match,
In the tree-tops the dicky-birds carolled,
All was peace – till I bungled that catch.

My attention the magic of summer,
Had lured from the game – which was wrong.
The bee (that inveterate hummer)
Was droning its favourite song.
I was tenderly dreaming of Clara
(On her not a girl is a patch),
When, ah, horror! There soared
through the air a
Decidedly possible catch.

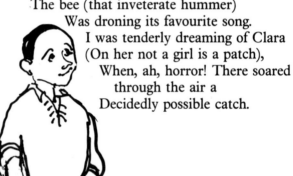

I heard in a stupor the bowler
Emit a self-satisfied 'Ah!'
The small boys who sat on the roller
Set up an expectant 'Hurrah!'
The batsman with grief from the wicket
Himself had begun to detach –
And I uttered a groan and turned sick. It
Was over. I'd buttered the catch.

Oh, ne'er, if I live to a million,
Shall I feel such a terrible pang.
From the seats in the far-off pavilion
A loud yell of ecstasy rang.
By the handful my hair (which is auburn)
I tore with a wrench from my thatch,
And my heart was seared deep with a raw burn
At the thought that I'd foozled that catch.

Ah, the bowler's low, querulous mutter
Points loud, unforgettable scoff!
Oh, give me my driver and putter!
Henceforward my game shall be golf.
If I'm asked to play cricket hereafter,
I am wholly determined to scratch.
Life's void of all pleasure and laughter;
I bungled the easiest catch.

P. G. Wodehouse

Wycombe Abbey Song

When the holidays are over, and the term is well begun,
When our lesson books are put away, and the morning's
work is done
Then we rush forth from the boot room, before the clock
strikes two,
For all of us are very keen to play lacrosse anew.
    Pass, catch, pass again, keep it in the air.
    Now the centre's caught it, so down the field we tear.

Now the hockey season follows and our sticks are routed
out,
When we've bullied at the centre, we begin to slash about.
We're fighting for our honour, for we want to win the
cup,
And the lusty shouts around us bid us not to give it up.
    HIC, HAC, HOC away, set it on the roll.
    Pass it down to somebody and quickly shoot a goal.

But the summer term is best for we are out from morn to
night,
Then we run out to play cricket as soon as it is light.
And we lie beneath the beeches when the sun is overhead,
Then cricket in the evening till it's time to go to bed.
    Slog, run, run again, you're running up the score.
    Now do look out for catches. How's that for leg before?

Anon

There's a Breathless Hush
in the Close Tonight
(Extract)

There's a breathless hush in the Close tonight –
Ten to make and the match to win –
A bumping pitch and a blinding light,
An hour to play and the last man in.
And it's not for the sake of a ribboned coat,
Or the selfish hope of a season's fame,
But his Captain's hand on his shoulder smote –
'Play up! Play up! and play the game!'

Sir Henry Newbolt

Play Ball

Okay, let's play, I think that we
Have everyone we need.
I'll be the strong-armed pitcher
Who can throw with blinding speed.
And Pete will be the catcher
Who squats low and pounds his mitt,
And Mike will be the home-run king
Who snarls and waits to hit
One, loud and long and hard and high,
Way out beyond the wall.
So let's get start – What? *You*? Oh, yes,
You can be the ball!

Shel Silverstein

Tribbling

There was a young fellow called Tribbling,
Whose hobby was basketball dribbling,
But he dribbled one day
On a busy freeway –
Now his sisters are lacking a sibling.

Dean Walley

Tonight I Feel like a Basketball Hero

Tonight I feel like a basketball hero
jumping to touch the reaching boughs
of trees which hang their baskets of summer leaves
over the pavement court.
Tonight in my new white canvas boots
I am silly and pleased
for no good reason that I can think of.
Tonight I am a basketball hero
chewing gum
putting one over the Harlem Globetrotters
making all them highschool queens
winning!

Jeff Cloves

The Wrestler's Complaint

A wrestler said: 'I'm in a spot!
The pace is becoming too hot!
   My opponent's unfair –
   He's pulled out my hair,
And tied both my legs in a knot.'

Frank Richards

Boxer Man in-a Skippin Workout

Skip on big man, steady steady.
Giant, skip-dance easy easy!
Broad and tall a-work shaped limbs,
a-move sleek self wid style well trimmed.
Gi ryddm yu ease of being strang.
Movement is a meanin and a song.
   Tek yu lickle trips in yu skips, man.
   Be dat dancer-runner man.

Yu so easy easy. Go-on na big man!
Fighta man is a ryddm man
full of de go, free free.
Movement is a dream and a spree.
Yu slow down, yu go faas.
Sweat come oil yu body like race horse.
   Tek yu lickle trips in yu skips, man.
   Be dat dancer-runner man – big man!

James Berry

I'm Gonna Destroy Joe Frazier

I'm gonna come out smokin'
And I won't be jokin'
I'm gonna be a peckin' and a pokin'
Pouring water on his smokin'
It might shock you and amaze ya
But I'm gonna destroy Joe Frazier

Muhammad Ali

Uncle 'Enery

Uncle 'enery
whose career in the ring
spanned almost two rounds
was a boxer of many parts.
He had: nerves of steel
       a will of iron
       a heart of gold
       a jaw of glass
alas.

Roger McGough

First Fight

Tonight, then, is the night;
Stretched on the massage table,
Wrapped in his robe, he breathes
Liniment and sweat
And tries to close his ears
To the roaring of the crowd,
A murky sea of noise
That bears upon its tide
The frail sound of the bell
And brings the cunning fear
That he might not do well,
Not fear of bodily pain
But that his tight-lipped pride
Might be sent crashing down,
His white ambition slain,
Knocked spinning the glittering crown.
How could his spirit bear
That ignominious fall?
Not he but a clown
Spurned or scorned by all.
The thought appals, and he
Feels sudden envy for
The roaring crowd outside
And wishes he were there,
Anonymous and safe,
Calm in the tolerant air,
Would almost choose to be
Anywhere but here.

Vernon Scannell

Last Fight

This is the one you know that you can't win.
You've lost your snap, can't put the punches in
The way you used to, belting till they fell;
You'll have a job to fiddle to the bell.
One round to go; backpedal, feint and weave;
Roll with the punches, make the crowd believe
You've still got something left. Above all, go
The distance, stay there till the end, although –
Even if you clipped him on the chin –
You know that this is the one that you can't win.

Vernon Scannell

The Fight of the Year

'And there goes the bell for the third month
and Winter comes out of its corner looking groggy
Spring leads with a left to the head
followed by a sharp right to the body
                daffodils
                primroses
                crocuses
                snowdrops
                lilacs
                violets
                pussywillow
Winter can't take much more punishment
and spring shows no signs of tiring
                tadpoles
                squirrels
                baalambs
                badgers
                bunny rabbits
                mad march hares
                horses and hounds

48

Spring is merciless
Winter won't go the full twelve rounds
        bobtail clouds
        scallywag winds
        the sun
        a pavement artist
        in every town
A left to the chin
and Winter's down!
        1 tomatoes
        2 radish
        3 cucumber
        4 onions
        5 beetroot
        6 celery
        7 and any
        8 amount
        9 of lettuce
        10 for dinner
Winter's out for the count
Spring is the winner!'

Roger McGough

Judo Contest

The novice grades had finished;
Now for the experts.
The tense, hot crowd around the mat
Hushed as the contestants appeared.
Strong, heavy men.
Black Belts.
Like jungle-cats they padded on to the soft mat.
The ceremonial bow. The starting position.
Like an explosion they started,
Concentration marking their features and feelings.
Their vice-like grips
Sliding along the damp, bare arm.
The agony of thinking many times faster than
    normal – new attacks
Different counters.
Their breath comes in short, sharp gasps
Like a vigorously-worked pump.
Their visions,
Distorted by the small streams of sweat that flowed
    down their bodies;
Their ankles,
Sore, stinging from the attempted ankle trips.

Quite suddenly a face lights up!
He can feel his opponent moving in
To throw.
A side-step.
A whip-like movement.
He's down – only his keen reflexes
Saved him from injury by breakfalling.
The bow of honour.

They quiver with relief and their release
From the nervous stress and strain.
Silently, exhaustedly,
They slip off the rough, damp, mat,
To rest and recover.

J. Rathbone

The Name of the Game

'Catch the ball!' the teacher cried.
I ran, I jumped, I stretched, I tried.
I really did.
  – I missed.

'Useless!' she yelled. 'Silly girl!' she spat.
'What on earth d'you think you're playing at?'
'A game,' I said.
  – And wept.

Jenny Craig

40 – Love

middle	aged
couple	playing
ten	nis
when	the
game	ends
and	they
go	home
the	net
will	still
be	be
tween	them

Roger McGough

Anyone For Tennis?

Anyone for tennis?
Go on, it's not really too wet.
I queued up all this morning,
These courts are hard to get.

Anyone for tennis?
You can have my brand-new racquet;
It's made of spaceship metal,
And it cost my dad a packet.

Anyone for tennis?
You can have my Tacchini top,
And I'll wear your rotten old T-shirt
From your mother's OXFAM shop.

Anyone for tennis?
You really cannot lose,
There's holes in both my trainers,
And you've got new Nike shoes.

Anyone for tennis?
Go on, just have a bash;
I'll do my service underarm,
And I promise not to smash.

Anyone for tennis?
I promise that you'll win,
Look, every ball that you hit back
I swear I'll call them In.

Anyone for tennis?
I'll give you fifteen-love each game.
Look, you can be Boris Becker,
And I'll be whatshisname.

Anyone for tennis?
What's the matter with you all?
Nobody's for tennis:
I'll play my friend the wall.

Richard Heller

Luke

Luke's a lisper.
I've heard whisper,
He's at his zenith
Playing tennith.

Colin West

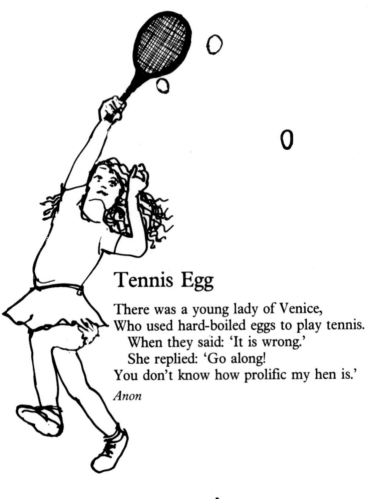

Tennis Egg

There was a young lady of Venice,
Who used hard-boiled eggs to play tennis.
   When they said: 'It is wrong.'
   She replied: 'Go along!
You don't know how prolific my hen is.'

Anon

Seaside Golf

How straight it flew, how long it flew,
It clear'd the rutty track
And soaring, disappeared from view
Beyond the bunker's back –
A glorious, sailing bounding drive
That made me glad I was alive.

And down the fairway, far along
It glowed a lonely white;
I played an iron sure and strong
And clipp'd it out of sight,
And spite of grassy banks between
I knew I'd find it on the green.

And so I did. It lay content
Two paces from the pin;
A steady putt and then it went
Oh, most securely in.
The very turf rejoiced to see
That quite unprecedented three.

Ah! Seaweed smells from sandy coves
And thyme and mist in whiffs,
In-coming tide, Atlantic waves
Slapping the sunny cliffs,
Lark song and sea sounds in their air
And splendour, splendour everywhere.

John Betjeman

Snorkelling

This strange and wavering shape I see –
Is it a friend or anenome?

William Cole

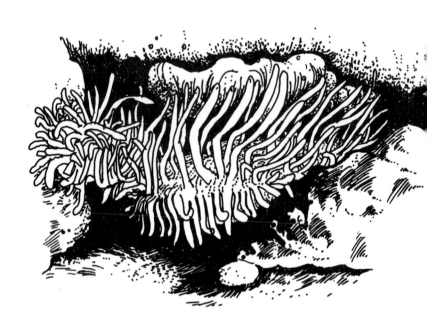

Fancy Dive

The fanciest dive that ever was dove
Was done by Melissa of Coconut Grove
She bounced on the board and flew into the air
With a twist of her head and a twirl of her hair.
She did thirty-four jackknives, backflipped and spun,
Quadruple gainered, and reached for the sun,
And then somersaulted nine times and a quarter –
And looked down and saw that the pool had no water.

Shel Silverstein

The Swimming Song

I like to swim
I'll meet you after school
It keeps us trim
I'll see you down the pool
It keeps us fit
Watch out we're on the prowl
We do our bit
Talcum powder and a towel
Both great and small
Watch us on the diving board
Life savers all
Duke of Edinburgh's Award
If we're around
We're demons in the drink
You won't get drowned
We never ever sink.

We swim like fish
Cod, kipper, cockle, carp
Here, there, gone, swish!
Oh play it on your harp
And diving too
In the deep dark dregs
Just me and you
We'll be laughing at the legs
Just name the stroke
Oh, the butterfly and crawl
And I'm your bloke
Will you give me back my ball?
I love to spring
Plunge plink plonk paddle
It makes me sing
Tra la diddle daddle.

We're in the shower
Shampoo soap scrub
For half and hour
Rub a dub a dub a dub
Do you know that
Dad gave me fifty pence
You aren't half fat
Ouch! Eeek! No offence!
It's great to swim
Never any pain or ache
It keeps us slim
Would you like a piece of cake?
So after school
If you have an hour to spend
Come to the pool
We'll race you to the end.

Pam Ayres

First Lesson

Lie back, daughter, let your head
be tipped back in the cup of my hand.
Gently, and I will hold you. Spread
your arms wide, lie out on the stream
and look high at the gulls. A dead-
man's float is face down. You will dive
and swim soon enough where this tidewater
ebbs to the sea. Daughter, believe
me, when you tire on the long thrash
to your island, lie up, and survive.
As you float now, where I held you
and let go, remember when fear
cramps your heart what I told you:
lie gently and wide to the light-year
stars, lie back, and the sea will hold you.

Philip Booth

The Diver

I put on my aqualung and plunge
Exploring, like a ship with a glass keel,
The secrets of the deep. Along my lazy road
On and on I steal –
Over waving bushes which at a touch explode
Into shrimps, then closing rock to the tune of the tide;
Over crabs that vanish in a puff of sand,
Look, a string of pearls bubbling at my side
Breaks in my hand –
Those pearls were my breath! .... Does that hollow hide

62

Some old Armada wreck in seaweed furled,
Crusted with barnacles, her cannon rusted,
The great *San Philip*? What bullion in her hold?
Pieces of eight, silver crowns, and bars of solid gold?

I shall never know. Too soon the clasping cold
Fastens on flesh and limb
And pulls me to the surface. Shivering, back I swim
To the beach, the noisy crowds, the ordinary world.

Ian Serraillier

Fishing

A line below a bridge,
                    Reflections blue –
The gasworks at your back,
                    A barge in view –
With not too many friends
                    And not too few –
A town canal is just the
                    Thing for you.

Mountains of junk below the
                    Surface hide –
Boys poling rafts and trailing
                    Ripples wide –
The grimy locks control a
                    Man-made tide –
A town canal with anglers
                    By its side.

Marian Lines

Fishing

Fishing, if I, a fisher, may protest,
Of pleasures is the sweetest, of sports the best,
Of exercises the most excellent;
Of recreations the most innocent;
But now the sport is marred, and wott ye why?
Fishes decrease, and fishers multiply.

Thomas Bastard (1566-1618)

The Angler's Lament

Sometimes over early,
Sometimes over late,
Sometimes no water,
Sometimes a spate,
Sometimes over thick,
And sometimes over clear.
There's aye something wrong
When I'm fishing here.

Anon

Catching a Fish

I have waited long with a rod
And suddenly pulled a gold-and-greenish,
Lucent fish from below,
And had him fly like a halo round my head,
Lunging in the air on the line.

Unhooked his gorping, water-horny mouth,
And seen his horror-tilted eye,
His red-gold, water-precious, mirror-flat bright eye;
And felt him beat in my hand, with his mucous, leaping
life-throb.

D. H. Lawrence

Fishing

Fishing all day long
and can't catch a thing.

What's wrong? What's wrong?
I ask the little worm
at the end of my hook.

The worm give me one look
and start to sing this song:

'Fish like to slip
in deep rain.
Not take a dip
in frying pan.'

John Agard

The Fish

I caught a tremendous fish
and held him beside the boat
half out of the water, with my hook
fast in a corner of his mouth.
He didn't fight.
He hadn't fought at all.
He hung on a grunting weight,
battered and venerable
and homely. Here and there
his brown skin hung in strips
like ancient wallpaper,
and its pattern of darker brown
was like wallpaper:
shapes like full-blown roses
stained and lost through age.
He was speckled with barnacles,
fine rosettes of lime,
and infested
with tiny white sea-lice
and underneath two or three
rags of green weed hung down.

While his gills were breathing in
the terrible oxygen
– the frightening gills,
fresh and crisp with blood,
that cut so badly,
I thought of the coarse white flesh
packed in like feathers,
the big bones and the little bones,
the dramatic reds and blacks
of his shiny entrails,
and the pink swim-bladder
like a big peony.
I looked into his eyes
which were far larger than mine
but shallower, and yellowed,
the irises backed and packed
with tarnished tinfoil
seen through the lenses
of old scratched isinglass.
They shifted a little, but not
to return my stare.
– It was more like the tipping
of an object toward the light.
I admired his sullen face,
the mechanism of his jaw,
and then I saw
that from his lower lip –
– if you could call it a lip –
grim, wet and weaponlike,
hung five old pieces of fish-line,
or four and a wire leader
with the swivel still attached,
with all their five big hooks
grown firmly in his mouth.
A green line, frayed at the end

Where he broke it, two heavier lines,
and a fine black thread
still crimpled from the strain and snap
when it broke and he got away.
Like medals with their ribbons
frayed and wavering,
a five-haired beard of wisdom
trailing from his aching jaw.
I stared and stared
and victory filled up
the little rented boat,
from the pool of the bilge
where oil had spread a rainbow
around the rusted engine
to the bailer rusted orange,
the sun-cracked thwarts,
the oarlocks on their strings,
the gunnels – until everything
was rainbow, rainbow, rainbow!
And I let the fish go.

Elizabeth Bishop

Seven fat fishermen

Seven fat fishermen,
Sitting side by side,
Fished from a bridge,
By the banks of the Clyde.

The first caught a tiddler,
The second caught a crab,
The third caught a winkle,
The fourth caught a dab.

The fifth caught a tadpole,
The sixth caught an eel,
But the seventh, he caught
An old cart-wheel.

Anon

Rowing

Swing the long oar
through the drifting water
See the waves breaking
in furls as we falter.
Curved is the blade
like the curve of a bow.
Swing your arms backwards
and forwards we go.

J. Stickells

A Sea Song

A wet sheet and a flowing sea,
A wind that follows fast
And fills the white and rustling sail
And bends the gallant mast;
And bends the gallant mast, my boys,
While like the eagle free
Away the good ship flies, and leaves
Old England on the lee.

O for a soft and gentle wind!
I heard a fair one cry:
But give to me the snoring breeze
And white waves heaving high;
And white waves heaving high, my lads,
The good ship tight and free –
The world of waters is our home,
And merry men are we.

There's tempest in yon horned moon,
And lightning in yon cloud;
But hark the music, mariners!
The wind is piping loud;
The wind is piping loud, my boys,
The lightning flashes free –
While the hollow oak our palace is,
Our heritage the sea.

Allan Cunningham

Eton Boating Song

Jolly boating weather
And a hay-harvest breeze,
Blade on the feather,
Shade off the trees;
Swing, swing together,
With your bodies between your knees.
    Swing, swing together,
    With your bodies between your knees.

Rugby may be more clever,
Harrow may make more row;
But we'll row for ever,
Steady from stroke to bow;
And nothing in life shall sever
The chain that is round us now.
    And nothing in life shall sever
    The chain that is round us now.

Others will fill our places,
Dressed in the old light blue;
We'll recollect our races,
We'll to the flag be true;
And youth will be still in our faces
When we cheer for an Eton crew.
    And youth will be in our faces
    When we cheer for an Eton crew.

Twenty years hence this weather
May tempt us from office stools:
We may be slow on the feather,
And seem to the boys old fools:
But we'll still swing together,
And swear by the best of schools.
       But we'll still swing together
       And swear by the best of schools.

William Cory Johnson

The Canoe-builder

There was a young man from Crewe,
Who wanted to build a canoe;
   He went to the river
   And found with a shiver,
He hadn't used waterproof glue.

Lorna Bain

Sea-fever

I must go down to the seas again, to the lonely sea and
the sky,
And all I ask is a tall ship and a star to steer her by,
And the wheel's kick and the wind's song and the white
sail's shaking,
And a grey mist on the sea's face and a grey dawn
breaking.

I must go down to the seas again, for the call of the
running tide
Is a wild call and a clear call that may not be denied;
And all I ask is a windy day with the white clouds flying,
And the flung spray and the blown spume, and the
seagulls crying.

I must go down to the seas again, to the vagrant gypsy
life,
To the gull's way and the whale's way where the wind's
like a whetted knife;
And all I ask is a merry yarn from a laughing fellow-
rover,
And quiet sleep and a sweet dream when the long trick's
over.

John Masefield

Haiku

Alone I cling to
   The freezing mountain and see
   White cloud – below me.

Ian Serraillier

Freddy

Freddy down the
Mountain skiing
Hit and killed a
Human being;
And to top this
Sad disaster,
Had to have his
Toe in plaster.

Colin West

A Prayer for Everest
(Before Climbing the Mountain)

That I may endure,
And love of friends confirm me;
That I lend my ear
Kindest to those who vex me;
That I may be strong,
My will guide the faint footsteps;
That heart and lung
May learn, rhythm is conquest;
That in the storm
My hand may stretch to help,
Not cringe in the glove to warm;
That courage of mine
Bring to friends courage too,
As I am brought by them;
That in the lottery
(My last, my worthiest prayer)
No envy bleed,
When, as I know my heart,
Others succeed.
Here be content, the thought;
I have done my part.

Wilfred Noyce

De Gustibus*

I am an unadventurous man,
And always go upon the plan
Of shunning danger where I can.

And so I fail to understand
Why every year a stalwart band
Of tourists go to Switzerland,

And spend their time for several weeks,
With quaking hearts and pallid cheeks,
Scaling abrupt and windy peaks.

In fact, I'm old enough to find
Climbing of almost any kind
Is very little to my mind.

A mountain summit white with snow
Is an attractive sight, I know,
But why not see it *from below*.

Why leave the hospitable plain
And scale Mont Blanc with toil and pain
Merely to scramble down again?

Some men pretend they think it bliss
To clamber up a precipice
Or dangle over an abyss,

To crawl along a mountain side,
Supported by a rope that's tied
– Not too securely – to a guide;

But such pretences, it is clear,
In the aspiring mountaineer
Are usually insincere.

And many a climber, I'll be bound,
Whom scarped and icy crags surround,
Wishes himself on level ground.

So I, for one, do not propose
To cool my comfortable toes
In regions of perpetual snows,

As long as I can take my ease,
Fanned by a soothing southern breeze
Under the shade of English trees.

And anyone who leaves my share
Of English fields and English air
May take the Alps for aught I care.

St John Emile Clavering Hankin

**from the Latin 'De gustibus non est disputandum' –
in matters of taste there can be no argument*

Skiing

Skiing is like being
part of a mountain.
On the early morning run
before the crowds begin,
my skis make
     little blizzards
as they plough
     through untouched powder
to leave fresh tracks
     in the blue-white snow.
My body bends and turns
     to catch each
bend and turn
     the mountain takes;
and I am the mountain
and the mountain is me.

Bobbi Katz

Patience

When skiing in the Engadine
My hat blew off down a ravine.
My son, who went to fetch it back,
Slipped through an icy glacier's crack,
And then got permanently stuck.
It really was infernal luck;
My hat was practically new –
I loved my little Henry too –
And I may have to wait for years
Till either of them reappears.

Harry Graham

Crampons are Useful when Climbing Mountains in Winter

Proud, alone,
Blown with wind,
Bleak it swathes the air
Like some defiant crag
Desperate with ice,
Shattered,
Battered with the icy blast.
Life clinging,
Dashed against the rocks,
Hard, unyielding,
Reaching into the steel blue sky
Shifting in the swirling grey
Gusts of bitter snow
Gusts of bitter sorrow,
Whirling, reeling,
Biting numb the feeling
This mountain's bigger than me.
Help.

Trevor Walters

The Midnight Skaters

The hop-poles stand in cones,
The icy pond lurks under,
The pole-tops steeple to the thrones
Of stars, sound gulfs of wonder;
But not the tallest there, 'tis said,
Could fathom to this pond's black bed.

Then is not death at watch
Within those secret waters?
What wants he but to catch
Earth's heedless sons and daughters?
With but a crystal parapet
Between, he has his engines set.

Then on, blood shouts, on, on,
Twirl, wheel and whip above him,
Dance on this ball-floor thin and wan,
Use him as though you love him;
Court him, elude him, reel and pass,
And let him hate you through the glass.

Edmund Blunden

Skateboard

Turning, banging, skating, diving,
Twisting, riding, slipping, sliding.
Zooming, whizzing, gliding, twisting,
Aching, pushing, pulling, lifting,
Skidding, spinning, riding, skateboarding.

Karen Howard (aged 10)

84

Skating
from The Prelude

And in the frosty season, when the sun
Was set, and visible for many a mile
The cottage windows blazed through twilight gloom,
I heeded not their summons: happy time
It was indeed for all of us – for me
It was a time of rapture! Clear and loud
The village clock tolled six, – I wheeled about,

86

Proud and exulting like an untired horse
That cares not for his home. All shod with steel,
We hissed along the polished ice in games
Confederate, imitative of the chase
And woodland pleasures, – the resounding horn,
The pack loud chiming, and the hunted hare.
So through the darkness and the cold we flew,

And not a voice was idle: with the din
Smitten, the precipices rang aloud;
The leafless trees and every icy crag
Tinkled like iron; while far distant hills
Into the tumult sent an alien sound
Of melancholy not unnoticed, while the stars
Eastward were sparkling clear, and in the west
The orange sky of evening died away.
Not seldom from the uproar I retired
Into a silent bay, or sportively
Glanced sideway, leaving the tumultuous throng,
To cut across the reflex of a star
That fled, and, flying still before me, gleamed
Upon the glassy plain; and oftentimes,
When we had given our bodies to the wind,
And all the shallowy banks on either side
Came sweeping through the darkness, spinning still
The rapid line of motion, then at once
Have I, reclining back upon my heels,
Stopped short; yet still the solitary cliffs
Wheeled by me – even as the earth had rolled
With visible motion her diurnal round!

William Wordsworth

Come Skating

They said come skating;
They said it's so nice.
They said come skating;
I'd done it twice.
They said come skating;
It sounded nice . . . .
I wore roller –
They meant ice.

Shel Silverstein

88

Esmé on Her Brother's Bicycle

One foot on, one foot pushing, Esmé starting off beside
Wheels too tall to mount astride,
Swings the off leg forward featly,
Clears the high bar nimbly, neatly,
With a concentrated frown
Bears the upper pedal down
As the lower rises, then
Brings her whole weight round again,
Leaning forward, gripping tight,
With her knuckles showing white,
Down the road goes, fast and small,
Never sitting down at all.

Russell Hoban

Beryl and her Bike

Ooh here comes Beryl such a sight
for sore cyclists' eyes
trim ankles turning blazing thighs
burning up the road
and miles ahead she shows
a clean pair of wheels
to all her trailing rivals
perfect on her perfect bike
Beryl always beats the clock
pure pleasure unalloyed is Beryl
for Beryl is the best yes
Beryl is the best

Beryl passes in a flash
chromey spokes Italian alloy gleam
lovely clean machine flown by
in a dazzling blink
yes in the pink is Beryl
for Beryl is the best
and evermore shall
be so

Jeff Cloves

*Beryl Burton – one of the UK's greatest athletes, has been
World Cycle Champion seven times and between 1958 and
1985 she was British Champion twenty-five times in succession.
She is still racing and winning.*

The Racer

I saw the racer coming to the jump,
Staring with fiery eyeballs as he rushed,
I heard the blood within his body thump,
I saw him launch, I heard the toppings crushed.

And as he landed I beheld his soul
Kindle, because in front he saw the Straight
With all its thousands roaring at the goal,
He laughed, he took the moment for his mate.

John Masefield

Hunter Trials

It's awf'lly bad luck on Diana,
Her ponies have swallowed their bits:
She fished down their throats with a spanner
And frightened them all into fits.

Now she's attempting to borrow.
Do lend her some bits, Mummy, *do*:
I'll lend her my own for tomorrow,
But today, *I'll* be wanting them too.

Just look at Prunella on Guzzle,
The wizardest pony on earth;
Why doesn't she slacken the muzzle
And tighten the breech in his girth?

I say, Mummy, there's Mrs Geyser
And doesn't she look pretty sick?
I bet it's because Mona Lisa
Was hit on the hock with a brick.

Miss Blewitt says Monica threw it,
But Monica says it was Joan
And Joan's very thick with Miss Blewitt,
So Monica's sulking alone.

And Margaret failed in her paces,
Her withers got tied in a noose,
So her coronet's caught in the traces
And now all her fetlocks are loose.

Oh, it's me now. I'm terribly nervous.
I wonder if Smudges will shy.
She's practically certain to swerve as
Her pelham is over one eye.

       *   *   *

Oh wasn't it naughty of Smudges?
Oh, Mummy, I'm sick with disgust.
She threw me in front of the Judges,
And my silly old collarbone's bust.

John Betjeman

Pegasus

First I rode a rocking horse,
Then I rode a bike – Oh,
They were very nice of course:
I know what I'd like though.

Pegasus lives down the lane;
We are secret cronies.
Mandy rides him now and then,
But she's bored with ponies.

Mandy calls him 'Hi!' or 'You!' –
Anything that's handy.
She doesn't know his real name though,
And he *belongs* to Mandy.

She tried him at a fence today:
It was pretty low too.
He simply stopped then walked away.
I said, 'He didn't throw you.'
'Useless thing,' she cried. 'No sense!
It might have been a show too.'

Everyday I hope she'll say
'Would you like to own him?
Take the silly thing away
Really I've outgrown him.'

But here's the secret no one knows;
That pony isn't idle.
In the night we rise in flight
No saddle and no bridle.
Through the air without a care
Higher still, and higher,
Don't you wish that you were there
Where Pegasus and I are?

Tam Lin

94

The Stallion

A gigantic beauty of a stallion, fresh and responsive to my
caresses,
Head high in the forehead, wide between the ears,
Limbs glossy and supple, tail dusting the ground,
Eyes full of sparkling wickedness, ears finely cut, flexibly
moving.

His nostrils dilate as my heels embrace him,
His well-built limbs tremble with pleasure as we race
around and return.

Walt Whitman

Rapping out loud
(Poet's note)

Raps are half-sung poems or half-spoken songs. Many of the best rappers make them up as they go along, but they must have a strong rhythm, which is why they are usually performed to music with the bass and drums dominating.

To say these raps, count out loud to a steady rhythm 'one and two and three and four and one and two and three and four' etc. Once you've got the rhythm going start rapping and fit the words to the beat. You'll find that sometimes the words fall on a number (an on-beat) and sometimes on 'and' (an off-beat).

Sometimes words like 'read it' are pushed together as 'read-it' and count as one beat and words like 'Zola' are broken into 'Zo–la' to count as two beats. It is less complicated than it seems and if you think of the way skipping rhymes work you'll soon get the hang of it.

The straight 4/4 beat above is the simplest form but raps can have various rhythms. Listen to Grandmaster Flash and other rappers on record to hear what can be done. Why not try writing your own?

Raps can be about anything, but they are particularly suitable for writing about things in the news, crazes and fashions. They work very well if you use slang and jargon – you could write a rap in computer language for example – and you can distort the way you say words to make them fit your rhythm.

If your rap has a chorus – try rapping it to a different rhythm to make it stand out.

HAPPY RAPPING!

After the Goldrush
Olympic Rap No. 1

I read it in the papers
heard it on the news
that little Zola
runs without shoes

She turned her ankle
tripped Mary up
so many a slip
twixt lip and cup

Stampeded in the goldrush
drowned in the flood
down goes Decker
and out goes Budd

Go for it gold diggers
going for gold
going for gold
going for gold

Jeff Cloves

* *Mary Decker (USA) and Zola Budd (GB),*
joint favourites for the 1500 metres – where
both failed to win medals when Decker fell.
(Los Angeles Olympics.)

Twice Daley
Olympic Rap No. 2

I do my daley dozen
take my daley vitamins
I practise daley habits
abstain from daley sins

I read the daley papers
to get my daley news
I watch the television
to get my daley views

I drink my daley Lucozade
when my daley work begins
I'm gonna do it daley 'cos
Daley Thompson always wins

Go for it twice Daley
going for gold
going for gold
going for gold

Jeff Cloves

* *Daley Thompson (GB) won his second decathlon gold medal in Los Angeles.*

Amazing Grace
Olympic Rap No. 3

I thought I saw Carl Lewis
sing on a TV show
I must have been mistaken
it turned out to be Grace Jones

He's so big so black so beautiful
his body's bought and sold
he's gonna make a million man
because he's solid gold

Go for it Carl
show them Russians good
that Moscow gold don't mean a thing
when you're bound for Hollywood

Go for it Carl
going for gold
Go for it Grace
going for gold
Jeff Cloves

* *Carl Lewis (USA) won four*
gold medals at Los Angeles and
was rumoured to be bound for
a showbiz career. The Russians
boycotted the LA games as the
Americans had boycotted the
Moscow games.

Soul Sisters
Olympic Rap No. 4

Look at Tessa Sanderson
throw that javelin
like a satellite in orbit
she puts it in a spin

From LA in the USA
she threw it high and far
and when at last it fell to earth
it made Tessa a star

She beat her greatest rival
from happiness she cried
then Fatima she pinched her cheek
and swallowed all her pride

Go for it soul sisters
going for gold
going for gold
going for gold

Jeff Cloves

* *Tessa Sanderson (GB) won the
javelin gold medal.
Fatima Whitbread (GB) was third.*

Cousin Fosbury

Cousin Fosbury
took his high-jumping seriously
To ensure a floppier flop
he consulted a contortionist
and had his vertebrae removed
by a backstreet vertebraeortionist

Now he clears 8 foot with ease
and sleeps with his head
tucked under his knees.

Roger McGough

Silly Races

There was a young man of Belfast,
Who ran in a race and came last;
He said: 'That's enough!
I'm all out of puff,'
As a tortoise came thundering past.

Carl Stevenson

Said a runner who raced in Argyll,
As he tried for the two-minute mile:
   'I know I can win it
   In less than a minute –
I'll just hang around for a while.'

E. O. Parrot

A rabbit raced a turtle,
You know the turtle won;
And Mister Bunny came in late –
A little hot cross bun.

Anon

The Ants at the Olympics

At last year's Jungle Olympics,
the Ants were completely outclassed.
In fact, from an entry of sixty-two teams,
the Ants came their usual last.

They didn't win one single medal.
Not that that's a surprise.
The reason was not for lack of trying
but more for their unfortunate size.

While the cheetahs won most of the sprinting
and the hippos won putting the shot,
the Ants tried sprinting but couldn't
and tried to put but could not.

It was sad for the Ants 'cause they're sloggers.
They turn out for every event.
With their shorts and bright orange tee-shirts,
their athletes are proud they are sent.

They came last at the high jump and hurdles,
which they say they'd have won, but they fell.
They came last in the four hundred metres
and last in the swimming as well.

They came last in the long distance running,
though they say they might have come first.
And they might if the other sixty-one teams
Hadn't put in a finishing burst.

But each year they turn up regardless.
They're popular in the parade.
The other teams whistle and cheer them,
aware of the journey they've made.

For the Jungle Olympics in August
they have to set off New Year's Day.
They didn't arrive the year before last.
They set off but went the wrong way.

So long as they try there's a reason.
After all, it's only a sport.
They'll be back next year to bring up the rear,
and that's an encouraging thought.

Richard Digance

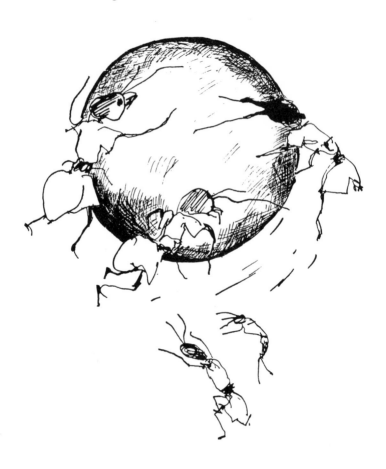

The High Jump

He slowly paced his distance off, and turned,
Took poise, and darted forward at full speed;
Before the bar the heavy earth he spurned,
Himself an arrow. They who saw his deed
Tensed muscles, poised and ran and leaped, and burned
With close-drawn breath, helping him to succeed:
Now he is over, they are over, too;
Foeman and friend were flying when he flew.

Anon

The Trampoline

You can weigh what you like for a trampoline,
Dear lady, for every additional ounce
The higher you go, if you see what I mean,
It's simply a question of bounce!
So here I go bouncing, dear lady, dear lady,
Bouncing, bouncing into the air.
You can land on your feet or alight on your bottom.
You soon get the knack of it. Never despair.
You can lilt like a lark in the morning, dear lady,
Or tumble and frolic and never feel sick.
All you must learn is the rhythm of bouncing,
Then you can perform every kind of a trick,
You can swallow-dive, somersault, spring on your palms,
You can dance funny dances aloft without qualms.
You can soar with the grace of a fairy queen,
Dear lady, you'll love the trampoline.

John Pudney

Dart Board Dance

I know,
it's been said before,
I ain't exactly slim!
I've been called
'a tub of lard',
and that's just to begin!

But deep inside this portly frame
looking far from neat,
lurks a natural athlete
that's never known defeat.

My game is darts
I'm an ace
my aim is straight and true
My hand is steady
as a rock,
my eyes are cool ice blue.

The room is dark and silent
everyone sits still
as I move in like a panther
ready for the kill.

I lay down my cigarette
I take a drink of beer
easing off the tension
as victory creeps near.

Double-top is needed
I have just one shot,
my dart is radar-guided
as it hits the spot.

Seb Coe eat your heart out
'cause you could be like me
Smoking fags and drinking beer
and tasting sweet victory.

Danny Pollock

Ping Pong

Swatted between bats
The celluloid ball
Leaps on unseen elastic
Skimming the taut net

Sliced   Spun
Screwed   Cut
Dabbed   Smashed

Point
Service

Ping   Pong
Pong   Ping
Bing   Bong
Bong   Bing

Point
Service

Ding   Dong
Dong   Ding
Ting   Tong
Tang   Tong

Point
Service

Angled   Slipped
Cut   Driven
Floated   Caressed
Driven   Hammered

Thwacked
Point
Service

Bit   Bat
Tip   Tap
Slip   Slap
Zip   Zap
Whip   Whap

	Point Service	
Left		Yes
Right		Yes
Twist		Yes
Skids		Yes
Eighteen		Seventeen
Eighteen		All
Nineteen		Eighteen
Nineteen		All
Twenty		Nineteen
	Point Service	
Forehand		Backhand
Swerves		Yes
Rockets		Yes
Battered		Ah
Cracked		Ah

SMASHED
SMASHED
SMASHED
GAME

Gareth Owen

111

'The Hurricane'

The chattering dies as the players walk in,
A handshake, a nod, and a smile.
Partisan feeling is almost a sin,
Earth stops in its course for a while.

The table is true and the cloth is as green
As pasture on Mid-Summer Day.
Where have they come from and what have they seen,
These giants who step out to play?

The opening frame, Alex Higgins to break,
These words have hardly been said,
Than Alex is up with the speed of a snake,
Kissed the blue and gone in off a red.

His opponent is careful and seizes his chance,
With some fine methodical play.
A push here, a nudge there and sometimes a glance,
His victory's well on the way.

He pots several blacks, an occasional pink,
Higgins' eyes have followed each shot,
Between smoking and puffing and taking a drink
He's wondering what chances he's got.

His opponent finally runs out of steam,
He's already scored fifty-eight.
His victory is now much more than a dream;
Higgins must swallow his fate.

Alex comes to the table with no sign of fear,
He knows just what he must do.
He can't get a red and the black is well clear,
So he snookers behind the blue.

His opponent is peering, but can't see the red,
He's been sipping his water, or gin,
Alex's snooker has left him for dead,
He doesn't know where to begin.

He misses and Alex pops up like a cork,
He's already striking the white.
He's just heard he's had a big winner at York,
It could be one hell of a night!

He puts down five reds, three blacks and a brown;
He's now got his sights on the blue.
If he gets it, they'll hear it way down in the town,
In Belfast and Manchester too.

Like a crack from a gun it flies into the sack,
There's only the colours to go.
One after another right down to the black,
They fall to each hurricane blow.

Snooker's played on 'the green', and it pays to be bold,
Each click of the balls sounds like cricket.
The crowd rise as they did to the Bradman of old,
When Hurricane 'comes to the wicket'.

John Jarvis

Confessions of a Born Spectator

One infant grows up and becomes a jockey,
Another plays basketball or hockey,
This one the prize ring hastes to enter,
That one becomes a tackle or centre.
I'm just as glad as glad can be
That I'm not them, that they're not me.

With all my heart do I admire
Athletes who sweat for fun or hire,
Who take the field in gaudy pomp
And maim each other as they romp;
My limp and bashful spirit feeds
On other people's heroic deeds.

Now A runs ninety yards to score;
B knocks the champion to the floor;
C risking vertebrae and spine,
Lashes his steed across the line.
You'd think my ego it would please
To swap positions with one of these.

Well, ego might be pleased enough,
But zealous athletes play so rough;
They do not ever, in their dealings,
Consider one another's feelings.
I'm glad that when my struggle begins
Twixt prudence and ego, prudence wins.

When swollen eye meets gnarled fist,
When snaps the knee, and cracks the wrist,
When calm officialdom demands,
Is there a doctor in the stands?
My soul in true thanksgiving speaks
For this most modest of physiques.

Athletes, I'll drink to you or eat with you,
Or anything except compete with you;
Buy tickets worth their weight in radium
To watch you gambol in a stadium,
And reassure myself anew
That you're not me and I'm not you.

Ogden Nash

The Runners

We're hopeless at racing,
Me and my friend.
I'm slow at the start,
She's slow at the end.

She has the stitch,
I get sore feet,
And neither one of us
Cares to compete.

But co-operation's
A different case.
You should see us
In the three-legged race!

Allan Ahlberg

Just When . . .

It's always the same.
Just when you're playing a game;
Just when it's exciting
And interesting
With everyone racing
And chasing,
Just when you're having so much fun,
Somebody always wants something done!

Max Fatchen

Acknowledgements

The editor and publishers would like to thank the following for permission to use copyright material in this collection. The publishers have made every effort to contact the copyright holders but there are a few cases where it has not been possible to do so. We would be grateful to hear from anyone who can enable us to contact them so the omission can be corrected at the first opportunity.

Edward Arnold Ltd for 'Patience' by Harry Graham from *Ruthless Rhymes for Heartless Homes*

Pam Ayres for 'The Swimming Song'

Bell and Highman Ltd for 'Rowing' by J. Stickells from *Poems for Movement*

James Berry for 'Quick Ball Man' and 'Boxer Man in a Skippin Workout'

The Bodley Head for 'Fishing' by John Agard from *I Din Do Nuttin*

Jonathan Cape Ltd for 'A Hero' by John Lane from *Fire Words* compiled by Chris Searle and 'Play Ball', 'Fancy Dive', and 'Come Skating' by Shel Silverstein from *A Light in the Attic*

Jeff Cloves for 'Beryl and her Bike', 'Tonight I Feel Like a Basketball Hero', 'Olympic Raps 1, 2, 3 & 4' and 'A Somerset CCC Shanty'

Ian Critchton Smith for 'Rhythm'

Jennifer Curry for 'The Name of the Game' by Jenny Craig

Curtis Brown Ltd for 'Confessions of a Born Spectator' © Ogden Nash

Andre Deutsch Ltd for 'Lizzie' and 'Here Are the Football Results' by Michael Rosen

Farrar Straus Giroux for 'The Fish' by Elizabeth Bishop

119

Ian Serraillier for 'Haiku: Alone I Cling to' from *I'll Tell You a Tale* (Puffin Books) and 'The Diver' from *Happily Ever After* (Oxford University Press)
The Society of Authors as the literary representatives of the Estate of John Masefield for 'The Racer' and 'Sea-Fever'
The Trustees of the Wodehouse Trust, A.P. Watt and Century Hutchinson Ltd for 'Missed' by P.G. Wodehouse
Watson, Little Ltd for 'The Old Field' by D.J. Enright from *Rhyme Time Rhyme* 1974
Kit Wright for 'The Rovers'

Index of titles

Index of authors